I LOVE You!

Around the World

I LOVE You!
Around the World

Lisa Swerling + Ralph Lazar

CHRONICLE BOOKS
SAN FRANCISCO

ARABIC (Egypt)

ENGLISH (Australia)

GAELIC (Scotland)

Tha gaol, agam ort!

SLOVENIAN

GREEK

Σ'αγαπώ!

HAWAIIAN

Aloha, au
ia 'oe !

TURKISH

ENGLISH (California)

Moi kon tan ou !

NEPALI

Kei te aroha au

Ki a koe !

ELEPHANT

ELVISH

كتيغيــــــــك !

MARTIAN (mars)

אני אוהב אותך!

Love, love me do!

DANISH

Jeg elsker dig!

TAIWANESE

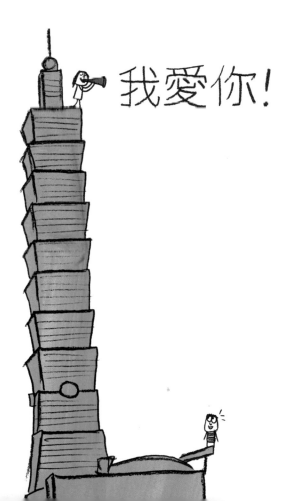

मुझे आपसे प्यार है!

FISH

GAELIC (Ireland)

KOREAN

딩신을 사랑합니다!

Adoro-te !

LATIN

Te amo!

Aš tave myliu !

GERMAN + FRENCH (switzerland)

Би чамд хайртай!

SPANISH (mexico)

Estoy enamorado de ti!

ROMANIAN

NORWEGIAN

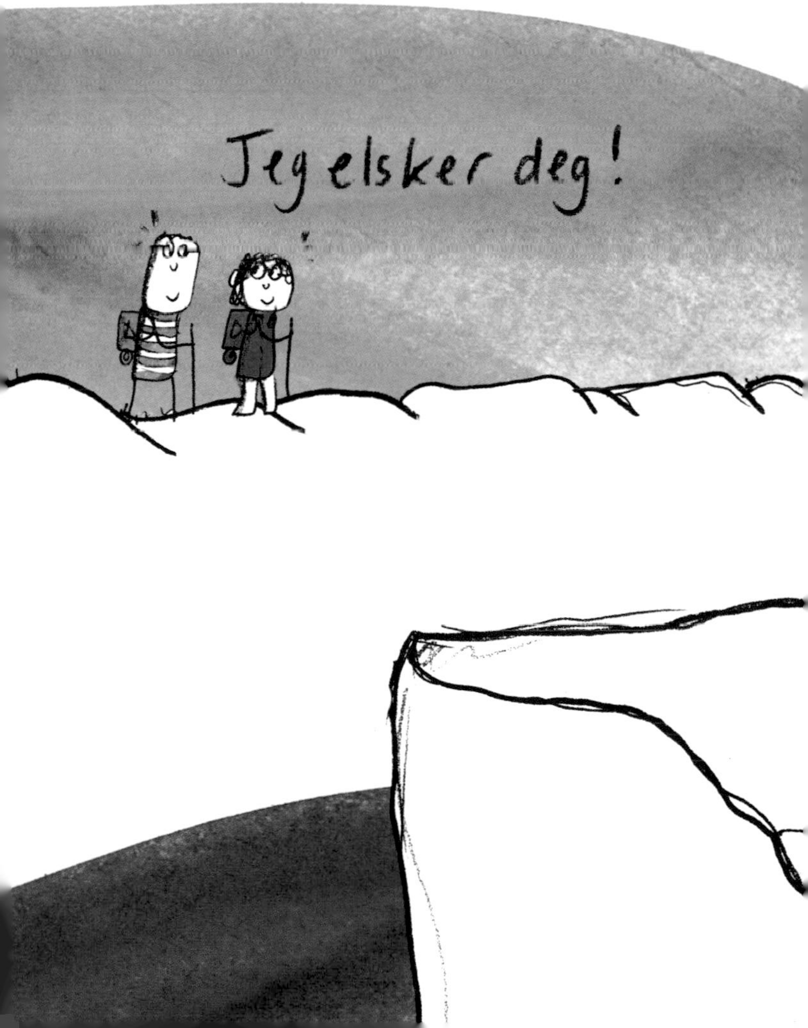

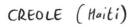
CREOLE (Haiti)

Mwen renmen ou!

SPANISH (Argentina)

Te quiero
mucho !

ARABIC

MALAGASY (Madagascar)

Tiako ianao!

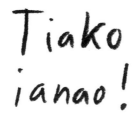

An domoni iko!

CROATIAN

SPANISH

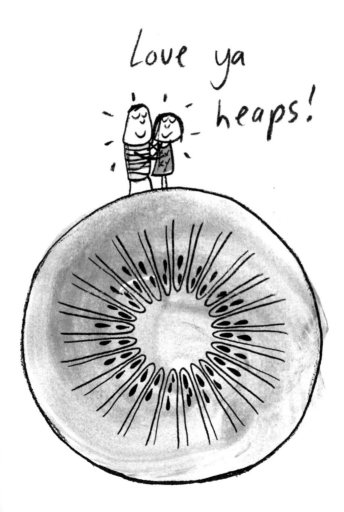

ENGLISH (Canada)

ฉันรัก คุณ !

CREOLE (Jamaican)

ISBN 978-1-4521-3601-1

MANUFACTURED IN CHINA

FSC
www.fsc.org
MIX
Paper from
responsible sources
FSC™ C104723

SPECIAL THANKS TO THE STAFF OF UNIVERSITY OF
CALIFORNIA, BERKELEY'S SOUTH AND SOUTHEAST ASIAN
STUDIES AND HYE-YOUNG YOON AT MIDDLEBURY
INSTITUTE OF INTERNATIONAL STUDIES AT MONTEREY
FOR HELP WITH TRANSLATIONS.

10 9 8 7 6 5 4 3 2 1

CHRONICLE BOOKS LLC
680 SECOND STREET
SAN FRANCISCO, CALIFORNIA 94107
WWW.CHRONICLEBOOKS.COM